D0725592

This book is a gift to:

_____

From:

_____

Date:

_____

199 Favorite Bible Verses for Men

© 2008 Christian Art Gifts, RSA
      Christian Art Gifts Inc., IL, USA

Designed by Christian Art Gifts

Images used under license from Shutterstock.com

Unless otherwise indicated, all Scripture quotations are taken from the *Holy Bible*, New International Version® NIV®. Copyright © 1973, 1978, 1984 by International Bible Society. Used by permission of Zondervan Publishing House. All rights reserved.

Scripture quotations marked NLT are taken from the *Holy Bible*, New Living Translation®, second edition. Copyright © 1996, 2004 by Tyndale House Publishers, Inc., Carol Stream, Illinois 60188. All rights reserved.

Scripture quotations marked NKJV are taken from the New King James Version. Copyright © 1979, 1980, 1982 by Thomas Nelson, Inc. Used by permission. All rights reserved.

Scripture quotations marked THE MESSAGE are taken from THE MESSAGE. Copyright © by Eugene H. Peterson, 1993, 1994, 1995, 1996, 2000, 2001, 2002 by NavPress Publishing Group. Used by permission.

Scripture quotations marked ESV are taken from the *Holy Bible*, English Standard Version. Copyright © 2001 by Crossway Bibles, a division of Good News Publishers. Used by permission. All rights reserved.

Scripture quotations marked KJV are taken from the *Holy Bible*, King James Version. Copyright © 1962 by The Zondervan Corporation. Used by permission.

Printed in China

ISBN 978-1-77036-121-8

15 16 17 18 19 20 21 22 23 24 – 30 29 28 27 26 25 24 23 22 21

199 favorite
Bible verses for
men

christian
art gifts ®

Contents

What to Do When I Need ...

Assurance 8

Confidence 11

Encouragement 14

God's Presence 17

Hope 20

Strength 23

Wisdom 26

What the Bible Says Concerning ...

Anger 30

Discipline 33

Family 36

God's Will 39

Humility 42

Integrity 45

Marriage 48

Priorities 51

Wealth 54

Rely on God for ...

The Future 58

Guidance 61

Help 64

Patience 66

Peace of Mind 69

Provision of Daily Needs 72

Success 75

God Freely Gives ...

Comfort 78

Courage 81

Forgiveness 84

Grace 87

Love 90

Mercy 93

Self-control 96

God Wants You To ...

Be Bold 100

Be Kind 103

Be a Leader 106

Be Modest 109

Pray 112

Persevere 115

Respect Others 118

Work 121

Worship 124

What to Do
When I Need ...

- 1 -

Since we have a great priest over the house of God, let us draw near to God with a sincere heart in full assurance of faith.

Hebrews 10:22

- 2 -

As far as the east is from the west, so far does He remove our transgressions from us.

Psalm 103:12 NKJV

- 3 -

The LORD is my light and my salvation – whom shall I fear? The LORD is the stronghold of my life – of whom shall I be afraid?

Psalm 27:1

- 4 -

"I tell you the truth, those who listen to My message and believe in God who sent Me have eternal life. They will never be condemned for their sins, but they have already passed from death into life."

John 5:24 NLT

- 5 -

"I am the LORD, your God, who takes hold of your right hand and says to you, 'Do not fear; I will help you.'"

Isaiah 41:13

There's no greater comfort than to remember that you're living in the center of God's will – nothing can ever happen to you without God's permission.
- Anonymous

Blessed assurance,

Jesus is mine!

Oh, what a foretaste

of glory divine!

Heir of salvation,

purchase of God,

born of the Spirit,

washed in His blood.

– Fanny Crosby

- 6 -

Being confident of this very thing, that He who has begun a good work in you will complete it until the day of Jesus Christ.

Philippians 1:6 NKJV

- 7 -

It is better to take refuge in the LORD than to trust in princes.

Psalm 118:9 NLT

- 8 -

The LORD will be your confidence and will keep your foot from being caught.

Proverbs 3:26 ESV

- 9 -

It is the LORD who goes before you. He will be with you; He will not leave you or forsake you. Do not fear or be dismayed.

Deuteronomy 31:8 ESV

- 10 -

So we say with confidence, "The Lord is my helper; I will not be afraid. What can man do to me?"

Hebrews 13:6

*Attempt great things for God,
expect great things from God.*
- William Carey

Oh, how great

peace and quietness

would he possess

who should cut off

all vain anxiety

and place all his

confidence in God.

— *Thomas à Kempis*

- 11 -

Do not let your heart faint, do not be afraid, and do not tremble or be terrified; for the LORD your God is He who goes with you, to fight for you against your enemies, to save you.

Deuteronomy 20:3-4 NKJV

- 12 -

If we are faithful to the end, trusting God just as firmly as when we first believed, we will share in all that belongs to Christ.

Hebrews 3:14 NLT

- 13 -

God equipped me with strength and made my way blameless. He made my feet like the feet of a deer and set me secure on the heights.

Psalm 18:32-33 ESV

May our Lord Jesus Christ Himself and God our Father, who loved us and by His grace gave us eternal comfort and a wonderful hope, comfort you and strengthen you in every good thing you do and say.

2 Thessalonians 2:16-17 NLT

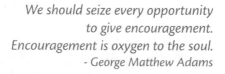

We should seize every opportunity to give encouragement. Encouragement is oxygen to the soul.
- George Matthew Adams

Encouragement

costs you nothing

to give, but is

priceless to receive.

– Anonymous

- 15 -

The LORD replied, "My Presence will go with you, and I will give you rest."

Exodus 33:14

- 16 -

You hide them in the shelter of Your presence.

Psalm 31:20 NLT

- 17 -

"Even to your old age and gray hairs I am He, I am He who will sustain you. I have made you and I will carry you; I will sustain you and I will rescue you."

Isaiah 46:4

- 18 -

"I am with you always, even to the end of the age."

Matthew 28:20 NKJV

- 19 -

"Behold, I stand at the door and knock. If anyone hears My voice and opens the door, I will come in to him and dine with him, and he with Me."

Revelation 3:20 NKJV

- 20 -

The LORD is near to all who call on Him, to all who call on Him in truth.

Psalm 145:18

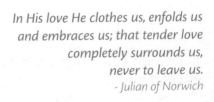

In His love He clothes us, enfolds us and embraces us; that tender love completely surrounds us, never to leave us.
- Julian of Norwich

What our Lord did was

done with this intent,

and this alone,

that He might be with us

and we with Him.

– *Meister Eckhart*

Hope

- 21 -

May the God of hope fill you with all joy and peace in believing, that you may abound in hope by the power of the Holy Spirit.

Romans 15:13 NKJV

- 22 -

For You, O LORD, are my hope, my trust, O LORD, from my youth.

Psalm 71:5 ESV

- 23 -

Let us hold fast the confession of our hope without wavering, for He who promised is faithful.

Hebrews 10:23 NKJV

- 24 -

So be strong and courageous, all you who put your hope in the LORD!

Psalm 31:24 NLT

- 25 -

Those who hope in the LORD will renew their strength. They will soar on wings like eagles; they will run and not grow weary, they will walk and not be faint.

Isaiah 40:31

- 26 -

Three things will last forever – faith, hope, and love.

1 Corinthians 13:13 NLT

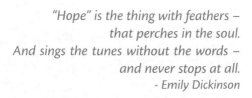

"Hope" is the thing with feathers –
that perches in the soul.
And sings the tunes without the words –
and never stops at all.
- Emily Dickinson

Make no little plans.

They have no magic

to stir men's blood.

Make big plans:

aim high in

hope and work.

– *Daniel Hudson Burnham*

- 27 -

"My grace is sufficient for you, for My strength is made perfect in weakness."

2 Corinthians 12:9 NKJV

- 28 -

God gives power to the faint, and to him who has no might He increases strength.

Isaiah 40:29 ESV

- 29 -

My health may fail, and my spirit may grow weak, but God remains the strength of my heart; He is mine forever.

Psalm 73:26 NLT

For You equipped me with strength for the battle; You made those who rise against me sink under me.

2 Samuel 22:40 ESV

God is my strength and power, and He makes my way perfect. He makes my feet like the feet of deer, and sets me on my high places.

2 Samuel 22:33-34 NKJV

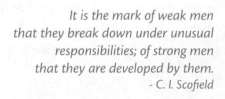

It is the mark of weak men that they break down under unusual responsibilities; of strong men that they are developed by them.
- C. I. Scofield

Do not pray for easy lives.

Pray to be stronger men!

Do not pray for tasks equal to

your powers. Pray for powers

equal to your tasks.

Then the doing of your work

shall be no miracle,

but you shall be a miracle.

– Phillips Brooks

Wisdom

- 32 -

If you need wisdom, ask our generous God, and He will give it to you. He will not rebuke you for asking.

James 1:5 NLT

- 33 -

To the man who pleases Him, God gives wisdom, knowledge and happiness.

Ecclesiastes 2:26

- 34 -

The fear of the LORD is the beginning of wisdom; a good understanding have all those who do His commandments. His praise endures forever.

Psalm 111:10 NKJV

- 35 -

The wisdom from above is first pure, then peaceable, gentle, open to reason, full of mercy and good fruits, impartial and sincere. And a harvest of righteousness is sown in peace by those who make peace.

James 3:17-18 ESV

- 36 -

Wisdom is sweet to your soul. If you find it, you will have a bright future, and your hopes will not be cut short.

Proverbs 24:14 NLT

- 37 -

Oh, the depth of the riches of the wisdom and knowledge of God! How unsearchable His judgments, and His paths beyond tracing out!

Romans 11:33

He is truly wise who

looks upon all earthly

things as folly that

he may gain Christ.

– *Thomas à Kempis*

What the Bible
Says Concerning ...

Anger

- 38 -

People with understanding control their anger; a hot temper shows great foolishness.

Proverbs 14:29 NLT

- 39 -

Refrain from anger and turn from wrath; do not fret – it leads only to evil.

Psalm 37:8

- 40 -

If possible, so far as it depends on you, live peaceably with all.

Romans 12:18 ESV

- 41 -

"In your anger do not sin": Do not let the sun go down while you are still angry.

Ephesians 4:26

- 42 -

Don't befriend angry people or associate with hot-tempered people, or you will learn to be like them and endanger your soul.

Proverbs 22:24-25 NLT

- 43 -

The LORD is compassionate and gracious, slow to anger, abounding in love. He does not treat us as our sins deserve or repay us according to our iniquities.

Psalm 103:8, 10

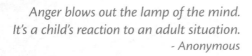

Anger blows out the lamp of the mind.
It's a child's reaction to an adult situation.
- Anonymous

Speak when you are angry

and you will make the best

speech you will ever regret.

– Ambrose Bierce

Discipline

- 44 -

No discipline is enjoyable while it is happening – it's painful! But afterward there will be a peaceful harvest of right living for those who are trained in this way.

Hebrews 12:11 NLT

- 45 -

Blessed is the man whom God corrects; so do not despise the discipline of the Almighty.

Job 5:17

- 46 -

Chasten your son while there is hope, and do not set your heart on his destruction.

Proverbs 19:18 NKJV

- 47 -

Discipline your children; you'll be glad you did – they'll turn out delightful to live with.

Proverbs 29:17 THE MESSAGE

- 48 -

Think about it: Just as a parent disciplines a child, the LORD your God disciplines you for your own good. So obey the commands of the LORD your God by walking in His ways and fearing Him.

Deuteronomy 8:5-6 NLT

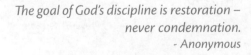

The goal of God's discipline is restoration – never condemnation.
- Anonymous

Discipline is the refining

fire by which talent

becomes ability.

– Roy L. Smith

Family

- 49 -

How great is the love the Father has lavished on us, that we should be called children of God! And that is what we are!

1 John 3:1

- 50 -

"Honor your father and mother. Then you will live a long, full life in the land the LORD your God is giving you."

Exodus 20:12 NLT

- 51 -

As a father has compassion on his children, so the LORD has compassion on those who fear Him.

Psalm 103:13

- 52 -

"Whoever does the will of God, he is My brother and sister and mother."

Mark 3:35 ESV

- 53 -

Train up a child in the way he should go, and when he is old he will not depart from it.

Proverbs 22:6 NKJV

- 54 -

"I will be a Father to you, and you will be My sons and daughters," says the Lord Almighty.

2 Corinthians 6:18

The most important thing a father can do for his children is to love their mother.
- Theodore Hesburgh

The family was ordained by
God before He established any
other institution, even before
He established the church.

– *Billy Graham*

God's Will

- 55 -

Trust in the LORD with all your heart, do not depend on your own understanding. Seek His will in all you do and He will show you which path to take.

Proverbs 3:5-6 NLT

- 56 -

Do not be conformed to this world, but be transformed by the renewing of your mind, that you may prove what is that good and acceptable and perfect will of God.

Romans 12:2 NKJV

- 57 -

The LORD directs the steps of the godly. He delights in every detail of their lives.

Psalm 37:23 NLT

- 58 -

The LORD says, "I will guide you along the best pathway for your life. I will advise you and watch over you."

Psalm 32:8 NLT

- 59 -

Give thanks in all circumstances; for this is the will of God in Christ Jesus for you.

1 Thessalonians 5:18 ESV

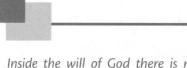

Inside the will of God there is no failure. Outside the will of God there is no success.
- Bernard Edinger

I find that doing

the will of God

leaves me with

no time for disputing

about His plans.

– George MacDonald

Humility

- 60 -

Humble yourselves in the sight of the Lord, and He will lift you up.

James 4:10 NKJV

- 61 -

"Whoever exalts himself will be humbled, and whoever humbles himself will be exalted."

Matthew 23:12

- 62 -

Don't be selfish; don't try to impress others. Be humble, thinking of others as better than yourselves. Don't look out only for your own interests, but take an interest in others, too.

Philippians 2:3-4 NLT

- 63 -

"Blessed are the meek, for they will inherit the earth."

Matthew 5:5

- 64 -

The reward for humility and fear of the LORD is riches and honor and life.

Proverbs 22:4 ESV

- 65 -

"Whoever humbles himself like this child is the greatest in the kingdom of heaven."

Matthew 18:4

If you plan to build a tall house of virtues, you must first lay deep foundations of humility.
- St. Augustine

Humility is not an ideal,

it is the unconscious

result of the life being

rightly related to God.

– *Oswald Chambers*

- 66 -

As for me, You uphold me in my integrity, and set me before Your face forever.

Psalm 41:12 NKJV

- 67 -

May integrity and honesty protect me, for I put my hope in You.

Psalm 25:21 NLT

- 68 -

May God Himself, the God of peace, sanctify you through and through. May your whole spirit, soul and body be kept blameless at the coming of our Lord Jesus Christ. The one who calls you is faithful and He will do it.

1 Thessalonians 5:23-24

- 69 -

Light is shed upon the righteous and
joy on the upright in heart.

Psalm 97:11

- 70 -

The LORD God is a sun and shield;
the LORD will give grace and glory;
no good thing will He withhold from
those who walk uprightly.

Psalm 84:11 NKJV

*Let unswerving integrity
ever be your watchword.
- Bernard M. Baruch*

Integrity: the virtue of

being good without

being watched.

– *Anonymous*

Marriage

- 71 -

He who finds a wife finds a good thing,
and obtains favor from the LORD.

Proverbs 18:22 NKJV

- 72 -

A man will leave his father and mother
and be united to his wife, and the two
will become one flesh.

Ephesians 5:31

- 73 -

Husbands, live with your wives in an
understanding way, showing honor
to the woman as the weaker vessel,
since they are heirs with you of the
grace of life, so that your prayers may
not be hindered.

1 Peter 3:7 ESV

- 74 -

May your fountain be blessed, and may you rejoice in the wife of your youth.

Proverbs 5:18

- 75 -

Let the husband render to his wife the affection due her, and likewise also the wife to her husband.

1 Corinthians 7:3 NKJV

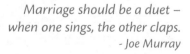

Marriage should be a duet –
when one sings, the other claps.
- Joe Murray

In a successful marriage,

there is no such thing as

one's way. There is only the

way of both, only the

bumpy, dusty, difficult,

but always mutual path.

– *Phyllis McGinley*

Priorities

- 76 -

"No one can serve two masters. Either he will hate the one and love the other, or he will be devoted to the one and despise the other. You cannot serve both God and Money."

Matthew 6:24

- 77 -

"Seek the Kingdom of God above all else, and live righteously, and He will give you everything you need."

Matthew 6:33 NLT

- 78 -

"Where your treasure is, there your heart will be also."

Matthew 6:21

- 79 -

"If anyone would come after Me, let him deny himself and take up his cross and follow Me. For whoever would save his life will lose it, but whoever loses his life for My sake will find it. For what will it profit a man if he gains the whole world and forfeits his life? Or what shall a man give in return for his life?"

Matthew 16:24-26 ESV

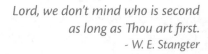

Lord, we don't mind who is second as long as Thou art first.
- W. E. Stangter

You can't get second things

by putting them first;

you can get second things

only by putting first things first.

— C. S. Lewis

- 80 -

It is a good thing to receive wealth from God and the good health to enjoy it. To enjoy your work and accept your lot in life – that is indeed a gift from God.

Ecclesiastes 5:19 NLT

- 81 -

"Seek first the kingdom of God and His righteousness, and all these things shall be added to you."

Matthew 6:33 NKJV

- 82 -

I have learned how to be content with whatever I have. I have learned the secret of living in every situation.

Philippians 4:11-12 NLT

- 83 -

Keep your life free from love of money, and be content with what you have.

Hebrews 13:5 ESV

- 84 -

Whoever trusts in his riches will fall, but the righteous will thrive like a green leaf.

Proverbs 11:28

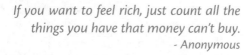

If you want to feel rich, just count all the things you have that money can't buy.
- Anonymous

The happiest of people

don't necessarily have

the best of everything.

They just make the

best of everything.

– Roy O. Disney

Rely on
God For ...

The Future

- 85 -

Many are the plans in the mind of a man, but it is the purpose of the LORD that will stand.

Proverbs 19:21 ESV

- 86 -

"For I know the plans I have for you," declares the LORD, "plans to prosper you and not to harm you, plans to give you hope and a future."

Jeremiah 29:11

- 87 -

The LORD will fulfill His purpose for me; Your steadfast love, O LORD, endures forever. Do not forsake the work of Your hands.

Psalm 138:8 ESV

- 88 -

Consider the blameless, observe the upright; there is a future for the man of peace.

Psalm 37:37

- 89 -

Don't brag about tomorrow, since you don't know what the day will bring.

Proverbs 27:1 NLT

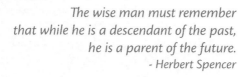

The wise man must remember
that while he is a descendant of the past,
he is a parent of the future.
- Herbert Spencer

The future has several names.

For the weak,

it is the impossible.

For the fainthearted,

it is the unknown.

For the thoughtful

and valiant,

it is the ideal.

– Victor Hugo

- 90 -

This God is our God for ever and ever;
He will be our guide even to the end.

Psalm 48:14

- 91 -

A man's heart plans his way, but the
LORD directs his steps.

Proverbs 16:9 NKJV

- 92 -

He will not let your foot slip – He who
watches over you will not slumber;
indeed, He who watches over Israel
will neither slumber nor sleep. The
LORD watches over you – the LORD
is your shade at your right hand; the
sun will not harm you by day, nor the
moon by night.

Psalm 121:3-6

- 93 -

The LORD says, "I will guide you along the best pathway for your life. I will advise you and watch over you."

Psalm 32:8 NLT

- 94 -

The steps of a man are established by the LORD, when He delights in his way.

Psalm 37:23 ESV

- 95 -

Show me Your ways, O LORD; teach me Your paths. Lead me in Your truth and teach me, for You are the God of my salvation; on You I wait all the day.

Psalm 25:4-5 NKJV

I am satisfied that

when the Almighty wants me

to do or not to do

any particular thing,

He finds a way

of letting me know.

— *Abraham Lincoln*

Help

- 96 -

I will lift up my eyes to the hills – from whence comes my help? My help comes from the LORD, who made heaven and earth.

Psalm 121:1-2 NKJV

- 97 -

God is our refuge and strength, an ever-present help in trouble.

Psalm 46:1

- 98 -

The LORD is my strength and my shield; in Him my heart trusts, and I am helped; my heart exults, and with my song I give thanks to Him.

Psalm 28:7 ESV

- 99 -

The LORD is good, a stronghold in the day of trouble; and He knows those who trust in Him.

Nahum 1:7 NKJV

God, who foresaw

your tribulation, has

specially armed you to

go through it, not without

pain but without stain.

– C. S. Lewis

Patience

- 100 -

Wait for the LORD; be strong and take heart and wait for the LORD.

Psalm 27:14

- 101 -

You also be patient. Establish your hearts, for the coming of the Lord is at hand.

James 5:8 NKJV

- 102 -

The Lord isn't really being slow about His promise, as some people think. No, He is being patient for our sake. He does not want anyone to be destroyed, but wants everyone to repent.

2 Peter 3:9 NLT

- 103 -

I waited patiently for the LORD; He inclined to me and heard my cry.

Psalm 40:1 ESV

- 104 -

Since God chose you to be the holy people He loves, you must clothe yourselves with tenderhearted mercy, kindness, humility, gentleness, and patience.

Colossians 3:12 NLT

Patience with others is love.
Patience with self is hope.
Patience with God is faith.
- Adel Bestavros

This would be a fine world

if all men showed as

much patience all the time

as they do while they're

waiting for the fish to bite.

– Vaughn Monroe

Peace of Mind

- 105 -

"I am leaving you with a gift – peace of mind and heart. And the peace I give is a gift the world cannot give. So don't be troubled or afraid."

John 14:27 NLT

- 106 -

I will both lie down in peace, and sleep; for You alone, O LORD, make me dwell in safety.

Psalm 4:8 NKJV

- 107 -

You will keep in perfect peace all who trust in You, all whose thoughts are fixed on You!

Isaiah 26:3 NLT

- 108 -

May the Lord of peace Himself give you His peace at all times and in every situation. The Lord be with you all.

2 Thessalonians 3:16 NLT

- 109 -

Let the peace of Christ rule in your hearts, since as members of one body you were called to peace. And be thankful.

Colossians 3:15

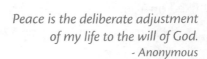

Peace is the deliberate adjustment of my life to the will of God.
- Anonymous

All things that

speak of heaven

speak of peace.

– Philip J. Bailey

- 110 -

"Your Father knows the things you have need of before you ask Him."

Matthew 6:8 NKJV

- 111 -

My God will meet all your needs according to His glorious riches in Christ Jesus.

Philippians 4:19

- 112 -

His divine power has granted to us all things that pertain to life and godliness, through the knowledge of Him who called us to His own glory and excellence, by which He has granted to us His precious and very great promises.

2 Peter 1:3-4 ESV

- 113 -

Don't forget to do good and to share with those in need. These are the sacrifices that please God.

Hebrews 13:16 NLT

- 114 -

He will give grass in your fields for your livestock, and you shall eat and be full.

Deuteronomy 11:15 ESV

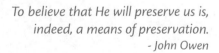

To believe that He will preserve us is, indeed, a means of preservation.
- John Owen

If God sends us

on stony paths,

He will provide us

with strong shoes.

– Alexander MacLaren

Success

- 115 -

Commit to the LORD whatever you do, and your plans will succeed.

Proverbs 16:3

- 116 -

"I know the thoughts I think toward you," says the LORD, "thoughts of peace and not of evil, to give you a future and a hope."

Jeremiah 29:11 NKJV

- 117 -

Whatever you do, work at it with all your heart, as working for the Lord, not for men, since you know that you will receive an inheritance from the Lord as a reward.

Colossians 3:23-24

- 118 -

It is not that we think we are qualified to do anything on our own. Our qualification comes from God.

2 Corinthians 3:5 NLT

- 119 -

May the LORD give you the desire of your heart and make all your plans succeed.

Psalm 20:4

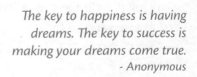

The key to happiness is having dreams. The key to success is making your dreams come true.
- Anonymous

God Freely
Gives ...

Comfort

- 120 -

Praise be to the God and Father of our Lord Jesus Christ, the Father of compassion and the God of all comfort, who comforts us in all our troubles.

2 Corinthians 1:3-4

- 121 -

"Blessed are those who mourn, for they shall be comforted."

Matthew 5:4 NKJV

- 122 -

"As a mother comforts her child, so will I comfort you; and you will be comforted."

Isaiah 66:13

- 123 -

"I will not leave you comfortless: I will come to you."

John 14:18 KJV

- 124 -

Cast your burden on the LORD, and He shall sustain you; He shall never permit the righteous to be moved.

Psalm 55:22 NKJV

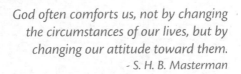

God often comforts us, not by changing the circumstances of our lives, but by changing our attitude toward them.
- S. H. B. Masterman

God does not

comfort us to

make us comfortable,

but to make

us comforters.

– J. H. Jowett

Courage

- 125 -

Be of good courage, and He shall strengthen your heart, all you who hope in the LORD.

Psalm 31:24 NKJV

- 126 -

"Be strong and courageous. Do not be frightened, and do not be dismayed, for the LORD your God is with you wherever you go."

Joshua 1:9 ESV

- 127 -

In Your strength I can crush an army; with my God I can scale any wall.

Psalm 18:29 NLT

- 128 -

"Fear not, for I am with you; be not dismayed, for I am your God; I will strengthen you, I will help you, I will uphold you with My righteous right hand."

Isaiah 41:10 ESV

- 129 -

Having hope will give you courage. You will be protected and will rest in safety.

Job 11:18 NLT

Courage is not the absence of fear, but rather the judgment that something else is more important than fear.
- Ambrose Redmoon

Courage is an

inner resolution to

go forward in spite

of obstacles and

frightening situations.

– Martin Luther King, Jr

- 130 -

If we confess our sins, He is faithful
and just to forgive us our sins and to
cleanse us from all unrighteousness.

1 John 1:9 ESV

- 131 -

"I will forgive their wickedness, and I
will never again remember their sins."

Hebrews 8:12 NLT

- 132 -

"Come now, let us reason together,"
says the LORD. "Though your sins are
like scarlet, they shall be as white as
snow; though they are red as crim-
son, they shall be like wool."

Isaiah 1:18

- 133 -

"If My people who are called by My name will humble themselves, and pray and seek My face, and turn from their wicked ways, then I will hear from heaven, and will forgive their sin and heal their land."

2 Chronicles 7:14 NKJV

- 134 -

"When you stand praying, if you hold anything against anyone, forgive him, so that your Father in heaven may forgive you your sins."

Mark 11:25

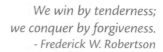

We win by tenderness;
we conquer by forgiveness.
- Frederick W. Robertson

We have a free, full, final, forever forgiveness in the atoning work of Christ.

– *J. Sidlow Baxter*

Grace

- 135 -

"My grace is all you need. My power works best in weakness."

2 Corinthians 12:9 NLT

- 136 -

Where sin increased, grace increased all the more.

Romans 5:20

- 137 -

God is able to make all grace abound toward you, that you, always having all sufficiency in all things, may have an abundance for every good work.

2 Corinthians 9:8 NKJV

- 138 -

God opposes the proud, but gives grace to the humble.

James 4:6 ESV

- 139 -

You know the grace of our Lord Jesus Christ, that though He was rich, yet for your sakes He became poor, so that you through His poverty might become rich.

2 Corinthians 8:9

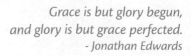

Grace is but glory begun,
and glory is but grace perfected.
- Jonathan Edwards

The word grace is
unquestionably the most
significant single word
in the Bible.

Love

- 140 -

"For God so loved the world that He gave His one and only Son, that whoever believes in Him shall not perish but have eternal life."

John 3:16

- 141 -

Show deep love for each other, for love covers a multitude of sins.

1 Peter 4:8 NLT

- 142 -

Love is patient, love is kind. It does not envy, it does not boast, it is not proud. It is not rude, it is not self-seeking, it is not easily angered, it keeps no record of wrongs. Love does not delight in evil but rejoices with the truth. It always protects, always trusts, always hopes, always perseveres. Love never fails.

1 Corinthians 13:4-8

- 143 -

"A new command I give you: Love one another. As I have loved you, so you must love one another. By this all men will know that you are My disciples, if you love one another."

John 13:34-35

- 144 -

I am persuaded that neither death nor life, nor angels nor principalities nor powers, nor things present nor things to come, nor height nor depth, nor any other created thing, shall be able to separate us from the love of God which is in Christ Jesus our Lord.

Romans 8:38-39 NKJV

Human love fails and

will always fail.

God's love never fails.

– Corrie ten Boom

Mercy

- 145 -

The LORD is gracious and full of compassion, slow to anger and great in
mercy. The LORD is good to all, and
His tender mercies are over all His
works.

Psalm 145:8-9 NKJV

- 146 -

Because of God's tender mercy, the
morning light from heaven is about
to break upon us, to give light to
those who sit in darkness and in the
shadow of death, and to guide us to
the path of peace.

Luke 1:78-79 NLT

- 147 -

To the LORD our God belong mercy
and forgiveness.

Daniel 9:9 ESV

- 148 -

God saved us, not because of the righteous things we had done, but because of His mercy.

Titus 3:5 NLT

- 149 -

"Blessed are the merciful, for they will be shown mercy. Blessed are the pure in heart, for they will see God."

Matthew 5:7-8

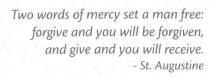

Two words of mercy set a man free:
forgive and you will be forgiven,
and give and you will receive.
- St. Augustine

Teach me to feel another's woe,

to hide the fault I see;

That mercy I to others show,

that mercy show to me.

– Alexander Pope

Self-control

- 150 -

Guard your heart above all else, for it
determines the course of your life.

Proverbs 4:23 NLT

- 151 -

God gave us a spirit not of fear but of
power and love and self-control.

2 Timothy 1:7 ESV

- 152 -

So think clearly and exercise self-control. Look forward to the gracious
salvation that will come to you when
Jesus Christ is revealed to the world.
So you must live as God's obedient
children. Don't slip back into your
old ways of living to satisfy your own
desires.

1 Peter 1:13-14 NLT

- 153 -

Make every effort to add to your faith goodness; and to goodness, knowledge; and to knowledge, self-control; and to self-control, perseverance; and to perseverance, godliness; and to godliness, brotherly kindness; and to brotherly kindness, love. For if you possess these qualities in increasing measure, they will keep you from being ineffective and unproductive in your knowledge of our Lord Jesus Christ.

2 Peter 1:5-8

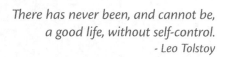

There has never been, and cannot be, a good life, without self-control.
- Leo Tolstoy

Self-control is more

often called for

than self-expression.

– *William M. Comfort*

God Wants
You To ...

Be Bold

- 154 -

So we may boldly say: "The LORD is
my helper; I will not fear. What can
man do to me?"

Hebrews 13:6 NKJV

- 155 -

Wait for the LORD; be strong, and let
your heart take courage; wait for the
LORD!

Psalm 27:14 ESV

- 156 -

"Be strong and courageous. Do not
be terrified; do not be discouraged,
for the LORD your God will be with
you wherever you go."

Joshua 1:9

- 157 -

"Fear not, for I am with you; be not dismayed, for I am your God. I will strengthen you, yes, I will help you, I will uphold you with My righteous right hand."

Isaiah 41:10 NKJV

- 158 -

Overwhelming victory is ours through Christ, who loved us.

Romans 8:37 NLT

*I am only one, but still I am one.
I cannot do everything,
but still I can do something;
I will not refuse to do the something I can do.*
- Helen Keller

Whatever you can do,

or dream you can, begin it.

Boldness has genius,

power, and magic in it.

- Johann von Goethe

Be Kind

- 159 -

But the Holy Spirit produces this kind of fruit in our lives: love, joy, peace, patience, kindness, goodness, faithfulness, gentleness, and self-control.

Galatians 5:22-23 NLT

- 160 -

Instead be kind to one other, tenderhearted, forgiving one another, as God through Christ forgave you.

Ephesians 4:32 NLT

- 161 -

Your kindness will reward you, but your cruelty will destroy you.

Proverbs 11:17 NLT

- 162 -

Make sure that nobody pays back wrong for wrong, but always try to be kind to each other and to everyone else.

1 Thessalonians 5:15

- 163 -

Whoever is kind to the needy honors God.

Proverbs 14:31

The person who sows seeds of kindness enjoys a perpetual harvest.
- Anonymous

Kindness makes a fellow

feel good whether it's being

done to him or by him.

– Frank A. Clark

Be a Leader

- 164 -

"Whoever wants to become great among you must be your servant, and whoever wants to be first must be slave of all. For even the Son of Man did not come to be served, but to serve, and to give His life as a ransom for many."

Mark 10:43-45

- 165 -

Let no one despise you for your youth, but set the believers an example in speech, in conduct, in love, in faith, in purity. Persist in this, for by so doing you will save both yourself and your hearers.

1 Timothy 4:12, 16 ESV

- 166 -

Work hard and become a leader.

Proverbs 12:24 NLT

He must manage his own family well and see that his children obey him with proper respect.

1 Timothy 3:4

He has told you, O man, what is good; and what does the LORD require of you but to do justice, and to love kindness, and to walk humbly with your God?

Micah 6:8 ESV

A good leader motivates, doesn't mislead, doesn't exploit. God cares about honesty in the workplace; your business is His business.

Proverbs 16:10-11 THE MESSAGE

Leaders who develop

people, add.

Leaders who develop

leaders, multiply.

– *John C. Maxwell*

Be Modest

- 170 -

Do not be rash with your mouth, and let not your heart utter anything hastily before God. For God is in heaven, and you on earth; therefore let your words be few.

Ecclesiastes 5:2 NKJV

- 171 -

Don't call attention to yourself; let others do that for you.

Proverbs 27:2 THE MESSAGE

- 172 -

God gives us more grace. That is why Scripture says: "God opposes the proud but gives grace to the humble."

James 4:6

- 173 -

Do not boast about tomorrow, for you do not know what a day may bring.

Proverbs 27:1 ESV

- 174 -

Pride ends in humiliation, while humility brings honor.

Proverbs 29:23 NLT

Great modesty often hides great merit.
- Benjamin Franklin

The Holy Spirit finds

modesty so rare that

He takes care to record it.

Say much of what the

Lord has done for you,

but say little of what you

have done for the Lord.

Do not utter a

self-glorifying sentence!

– *Charles H. Spurgeon*

Pray

- 175 -

The earnest prayer of a righteous person has great power and produces wonderful results.

James 5:16 NLT

- 176 -

The LORD is near to all who call on Him, to all who call on Him in truth. He fulfills the desires of those who fear Him; He hears their cry and saves them.

Psalm 145:18-19

- 177 -

"Whatever you ask in prayer, you will receive, if you have faith."

Matthew 21:22 ESV

- 178 -

"But when you pray, go into your room, close the door and pray to your Father, who is unseen. Then your Father, who sees what is done in secret, will reward you."

Matthew 6:6

- 179 -

"I say to you, whatever things you ask when you pray, believe that you receive them, and you will have them."

Mark 11:24 NKJV

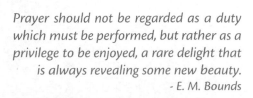

Prayer should not be regarded as a duty which must be performed, but rather as a privilege to be enjoyed, a rare delight that is always revealing some new beauty.
- E. M. Bounds

The men who have

done the most

for God in this

world have been early

on their knees.

— E. M. Bounds

Persevere

- 180 -

Blessed is the man who endures temptation; for when he has been approved, he will receive the crown of life which the Lord has promised to those who love Him.

James 1:12 NKJV

- 181 -

Therefore, my beloved brothers, be steadfast, immovable, always abounding in the work of the Lord, knowing that in the Lord your labor is not in vain.

1 Corinthians 15:58 ESV

- 182 -

"The one who endures to the end will be saved."

Matthew 24:13 NLT

- 183 -

Not only so, but we also rejoice in our sufferings, because we know that suffering produces perseverance; perseverance, character; and character, hope. And hope does not disappoint us, because God has poured out His love into our hearts by the Holy Spirit, whom He has given us.

Romans 5:3-5

- 184 -

"Because you have obeyed My command to persevere, I will protect you from the great time of testing that will come upon the whole world to test those who belong to this world."

Revelation 3:10 NLT

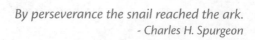

By perseverance the snail reached the ark.
- Charles H. Spurgeon

Our motto must continue

to be perseverance.

And ultimately I trust

the Almighty will crown

our efforts with success.

– William Wilberforce

- 185 -

Do nothing out of selfish ambition or vain conceit, but in humility consider others better than yourselves.

Philippians 2:3

- 186 -

You, dear friends, must build each other up in your most holy faith, pray in the power of the Holy Spirit.

Jude 20 NLT

- 187 -

Honor your father and your mother, so that you may live long in the land the LORD your God is giving you.

Exodus 20:12

- 188 -

Pay to all what is owed to them: taxes to whom taxes are owed, revenue to whom revenue is owed, respect to whom respect is owed, honor to whom honor is owed.

Romans 13:7 ESV

- 189 -

Show proper respect to everyone: Love the brotherhood of believers.

1 Peter 2:17

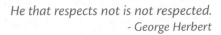

He that respects not is not respected.
- George Herbert

Without respect,

love cannot go

far or rise high:

it is an angel with

but one wing.

– *Alexandre Dumas*

Work

- 190 -

Whatever you do, work at it with all your heart, as working for the Lord, not for men, since you know that you will receive an inheritance from the Lord as a reward. It is the Lord Christ you are serving.

Colossians 3:23-24

- 191 -

His lord said to him, "Well done, good and faithful servant; you have been faithful over a few things, I will make you ruler over many things. Enter into the joy of your lord."

Matthew 25:23 NKJV

- 192 -

Do your best to present yourself to God as one approved, a worker who has no need to be ashamed, rightly handling the word of truth.

2 Timothy 2:15 ESV

- 193 -

The LORD will open the heavens, the storehouse of His bounty, to send rain on your land in season and to bless all the work of your hands.

Deuteronomy 28:12

- 194 -

"Take My yoke upon you, and learn from Me, for I am gentle and lowly in heart, and you will find rest for your souls. For My yoke is easy, and My burden is light."

Matthew 11:29-30 ESV

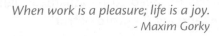

When work is a pleasure; life is a joy.
- Maxim Gorky

For anything worth having

one must pay the price;

and the price is always work,

patience, love, self-sacrifice.

– John Burroughs

Worship

- 195 -

"God is spirit, and His worshipers must worship in spirit and in truth."

John 4:24

- 196 -

Honor the LORD for the glory of His name. Worship the LORD in the splendor of His holiness.

Psalm 29:2 NLT

- 197 -

So here's what I want you to do, God helping you: Take your everyday, ordinary life – your sleeping, eating, going-to-work, and walking-around life – and place it before God as an offering. Embracing what God does for you is the best thing you can do for Him.

Romans 12:1 THE MESSAGE

- 198 -

I praise You because I am fearfully and wonderfully made; Your works are wonderful, I know that full well.

Psalm 139:14

- 199 -

For great is the LORD, and greatly to be praised, and He is to be held in awe above all gods.

1 Chronicles 16:25 ESV

The more a man bows his knee before God, the straighter he stands before men.
- Anonymous

It is only when men

begin to worship

that they begin to grow.

– Calvin Coolidge

Notes